UNCOVERING THE PAST:
ANALYZING PRIMARY SOURCES

THE UNDERGROUND RAILROAD

NATALIE HYDE

Crabtree Publishing Company
www.crabtreebooks.com

Author: Natalie Hyde
**Publishing plan research and
   development:** Reagan Miller
Editor-in-Chief: Lionel Bender
Editors: Simon Adams, Anastasia Suen
Proofreaders: Laura Booth,
   Wendy Scavuzzo
Project coordinator: Kelly Spence
Design and photo research: Ben White
Production: Kim Richardson
**Production coordinator and
   prepress technician:** Ken Wright
Print coordinator: Margaret Amy Salter

Consultant: Amie Wright,
The New York Public Library

This book was produced for
Crabtree Publishing Company by
Bender Richardson White

Photographs and reproductions:
Front Cover: Wikimedia Commons: (William H. Cheney, South Orange, NJ)
Interior: Corbis: 26–27 middle (National Geographic Society/Corbis). Getty Images: 38–39 (Andrew Burton/Getty Images); 41 bottom (Education Images/Getty Images). Library of Congress: 1 middle (LC-DIG-stereo-1s02415); 3 Btm Mid (LC-USZ62-7816); 4 top left (Icon) (LC-USZC4-62799); 6 top left (Icon) (LC-USZ62-62799); 8 top left (LC-USZC4-6677); 10 top left (LC-USZC4-6677); 11 bottom right (LC-B8171-3608); 12 top left (LC-USZC4-6677); 13 top (LC-DIG-stereo-1s02415); 14 top left (LC-USZC4-6677); 14–15 middle (LC-USZ62-98515); 16 top left (LC-USZ62-75975); 18 top left (LC-USZ62-75975); 20 top left (LC-DIG-stereo-1s02891); 22 top left (LC-DIG-stereo-1s02891); 24 top left (LC-DIG-stereo-1s02891); 25 middle (LC-DIG-stereo-1s02891); 26 top left (LC-DIG-stereo-1s02891); 27 top right (LC-USZ62-7816); 28 top left (LC-DIG-stereo-1s02891); 30 top left (LC-DIG-stereo-1s02891); 31 bottom (LC-USZCN4-225); 32 top left (LC-USZC4-10315); 34 top left (LC-USZC4-10315); 35 top right (LC-USZC4-5950); 36 top left (LC-USZC4-10315); 36-37 middle (LC-USZ62-91379); 38 top left (LC-DIG-stereo-1s02415); 40 top left (LC-DIG-stereo-1s02415). Shutterstock.com: 1 full page (Petrov Stanislav). Topfoto: 4-5 (The Granger Collection–G.C.); 6 middle right (World History Archive); 7 top right (G.C.); 8–9 (G.C.); 10–11 bottom (G.C.); 13 bottom (G.C.); 15 middle right (G.C.); 16–17 (G.C.); 18 top right (G.C.); 19 (G.C.); 20–21 (G.C.); 22–23 middle (G.C.); 23 right (G.C.); 24 middle right (G.C.); 28 middle right (G.C.); 29 top right (G.C.); 29 middle (Topham Picturepoint); 31 top left (Charles Phelps Cushing/ClassicStock); 32–33 World History Archive); 34 middle right (G.C.); 37 top right (G.C.); 40 middle right (G.C.). Map: Stefan Chabluk.

Library and Archives Canada Cataloguing in Publication

Hyde, Natalie, 1963-, author
   The Underground Railroad / Natalie Hyde.

(Uncovering the past: analyzing primary sources)
Includes index.
Issued in print and electronic formats.
ISBN 978-0-7787-1551-1 (bound).--
ISBN 978-0-7787-1555-9 (pbk.).--
ISBN 978-1-4271-1603-1 (pdf).--ISBN 978-1-4271-1599-7 (html)

      1. Underground Railroad--Juvenile literature. 2.
Underground Railroad--Sources--Juvenile literature. I. Title.

E450.H93 2015   j973.7'115   C2014-908087-5
                                           C2014-908088-3

Library of Congress Cataloging-in-Publication Data

Hyde, Natalie, 1963-
   The Underground Railroad / Natalie Hyde.
      pages cm. -- (Uncovering the past: analyzing primary sources)
   Includes index.
   ISBN 978-0-7787-1551-1 (library binding : alk. paper) --
   ISBN 978-0-7787-1555-9 (pbk. : alk. paper) --
   ISBN 978-1-4271-1603-1 (pdf : alk. paper) --
   ISBN 978-1-4271-1599-7 (html : alk. paper)
   1. Underground Railroad--Juvenile literature. 2. Fugitive slaves--United States--Juvenile literature. I. Title.

   E450.F533 2015
   973.7'115--dc23
                                           2014046706

Crabtree Publishing Company
www.crabtreebooks.com   1-800-387-7650

Copyright © **2015 CRABTREE PUBLISHING COMPANY.** All rights reserved. No part of this publication may be reproduced, stored in a retrieval system or be transmitted in any form or by any means, electronic, mechanical, photocopying, recording, or otherwise, without the prior written permission of Crabtree Publishing Company. In Canada: We acknowledge the financial support of the Government of Canada through the Canada Book Fund for our publishing activities.

Printed in Canada/022015/MA20150101

Published in Canada
Crabtree Publishing
616 Welland Ave.
St. Catharines, ON
L2M 5V6

Published in the United States
Crabtree Publishing
PMB 59051
350 Fifth Avenue, 59th Floor
New York, NY 10118

Published in the United Kingdom
Crabtree Publishing
Maritime House
Basin Road North, Hove
BN41 1WR

Published in Australia
Crabtree Publishing
3 Charles Street
Coburg North
VIC, 3058

UNCOVERING THE PAST:
ANALYZING PRIMARY SOURCES

THE PAST COMES ALIVE

"Those who cannot remember the past are condemned to repeat it."

George Santayana, 19th-century U.S. philosopher

The Underground Railroad is part of the story of slavery in the United States and Canada from 1840 to 1860. Uncovering this historical event and the people and places involved required sourcing, analyzing, and interpreting **evidence** from the past.

The past is time that has gone by and no longer exists. It is also a series of events. The events that happen in the past are called **history**. Some events create a sense of pride in what we have achieved, while some we look back on with shame. Important events, whether good or bad, reveal the truth about a people and help to show us their **culture** and **beliefs**. By studying the past, we learn about others and learn about ourselves. We learn what works in **society**, what does not, and what things cause people or society to change. By remembering the past, we can try to avoid making the same mistakes.

DEFINITIONS

Historical time can be described by the number of years or events:

A **decade** is a period of 10 years, a **century** 100 years, and a **millennium** 1,000 years.

A **generation** is all the people born and living at the same time, such as the Baby Boomers (1946 — 1964).

An **era** is a period with a distinct **characteristic**, such as the longterm economic prosperity of the Roaring Twenties (1920s).

An **age** is a long era, such as the Elizabethan Age (1558 — 1603).

▼ In America, slaves were often sold at markets or **auctions**. They had no say in what happened to them. Women were sold to be cooks and housekeepers.

EVIDENCE RECORD CARD

A slave auction in Virginia
LEVEL Primary source
MATERIAL Oil on canvas painting
    Painter: Eyre Crowe
LOCATION Richmond, Virginia
DATE 1852–1853
SOURCE The Granger Collection

INTRODUCTION

HOW DO WE LEARN ABOUT OUR HISTORY?

Before humans used written language, storytellers passed down tales of heroes, tragedies, and other historic events **orally**. Images found in caves show that sometimes ancient peoples used paintings or carvings to depict aspects of their lives. Architecture, tools, and everyday utensils also give clues to past cultures.

Once written language was created, the record of our past grew with accounts of events available to more than one generation at a time.

Images let us look into the past through either an artist's eyes or camera's lens. Painters and sculptors in ancient Egypt, for example, showed us what Egyptians wore in clothing, jewelry, and make-up.

We can also learn about our past by interviewing other people who were involved in, witnessed, or knew someone who was affected by important events.

A **historian** is a person who studies history. Often a historian specializes in a particular time period, region of the world, subject matter, or certain event. Historians are important because they research what has happened in the past and gather the information to develop theories about why something happened and what effect it had on society.

▶ Slave ships were large ships that originally carried cargo but were converted to transport slaves.

PERSPECTIVES

This ship plan shows the different deck levels of a ship and their usage. What does this tell you about conditions on a slave ship for the slaves? What does this image show you about how slaves were regarded?

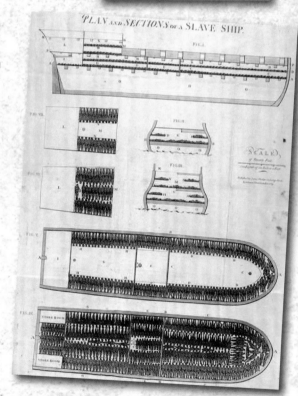

PLAN AND SECTIONS OF A SLAVE SHIP.

"She asked me to come in, loaded a plate with venison and bread, and, when I laid it into my handkerchief, and put a quarter of a dollar on the table, she quietly took it up and put it in my handkerchief, with an additional quantity of venison. I felt the hot tears roll down my cheeks as she said, 'God bless you;' and I hurried away to bless my starving wife and little ones."

Excerpt from *Truth Stranger Than Fiction* by Josiah Henson

Finding information is not always easy for historians. They have to look hard to uncover certain types of written or picture evidence.

Historians researching the Underground Railroad have great difficulty finding material because the whole operation was kept highly secret to protect those people involved. Very few records were kept, because it was dangerous for the **fugitives**—escapees or those in hiding—and for their protectors, if they were found.

▼ As many as 20 million Africans were transported on slave ships to North America.

ANALYZE THIS

The Underground Railroad affected the lives of thousands of people. Why then are there so few records of this time in history for historians to find?

TYPES OF EVIDENCE

"Information is a source of learning. But unless it is organized, processed, and available to the right people in a format for decision making, it is a burden, not a benefit."

C. William Pollard, U.S. businessman

A **source** is a book, statement, person, or image that supplies information. Historical source material can be found in libraries, museums, archives, and private collections.

Source material is important because it brings us as close to the past as we can get without being there. Journal entries, photographs, and **audio recordings** can portray more than information—they can relate the emotion of the event.

By looking at source material, you can come to your own conclusions about something instead of relying on someone else's opinion.

Historical sources can be **preserved** on purpose or accidentally. If the value of the source is recognized, it will likely be kept in a safe, or donated to a museum, or stored carefully in an attic. Some source material is not knowingly preserved. Old newspapers might be used to wrap fragile china or used as insulation in walls. Later on, the information in the newspapers might shed light on important events or family trees.

"My poor sister was sold first: she was knocked down to a planter who resided at some distance in the country. Then I was called upon the stand. While the auctioneer was crying the bids, I saw the man that had purchased my sister getting her into a cart, to take her to his home."

Excerpt from *Running a Thousand Miles for Freedom* by William and Ellen Craft

SUNNY SOUTH

ANALYZE THIS

If this painting were the only source material you saw on the subject of slavery in the United States, what conclusion would you draw? Would you think slaves lived a brutal life of hard labor, or would you think they had a peaceful, happy existence?

◀ This oil painting from c. 1883 would have been an expensive piece of artwork in its plantation home. Many such paintings survived because they were carefully preserved and passed down through the generations.

PRIMARY SOURCES OF INFORMATION

A **primary source** is a first-hand account, record, or direct evidence of an event. It is often created at the time of the event. Primary sources can be many different types of historical material, including **auditory**, written, or visual **artifacts**.

Written primary sources can give more information than just the words. The handwriting, paper, ink, mistakes or corrections, and even margin notes, can all add to our knowledge about the time, place, or **circumstances** of its creation. Elegant handwriting and good grammar suggest a higher education. Tears from crying leave salt stains on paper. Fire or smoke can damage the edges of a page. Notes in margins can hint at the frame of mind of the person commenting on or reading the document.

▼ In auction houses, slaves would be kept in pens until called. They then stood on a platform at one end of the room so they could be seen and inspected by the buyers.

Primary written sources can be:
- Diaries: Books where someone keeps private personal information
- Journals: Written accounts of a period of time or a journey
- Letters: Written communications sent by mail or messenger
- Broadsides: Leaflets advertising something
- Autobiographies: Stories of someone's life, written by that person
- Books: Pages of stories or information bound together
- **Lyrics**: The words to poems, songs, or church hymns

"[William] had been sold once one sister had been sold also. He was prompted to escape because he wanted his liberty—was not satisfied with not having the priviledge of providing for his family, His value $1000-. Paid $240-for himself, wife & child & Mrs Bell."

Excerpt from diary of William Still, June 22, 1855

- Blogs: Online journals
- **Social media** posts: Updates on social media sites such as Facebook or Twitter

Primary written source material for the Underground Railroad includes newspaper articles and advertisements, broadsides, letters, journals, and official records.

Artifacts can also be seen as primary sources. Items such as war **memorabilia**, medals, and badges, as well as needlework, jewelry, leather goods, cards, and board games can give us an **insight** into people's lives and their accomplishments.

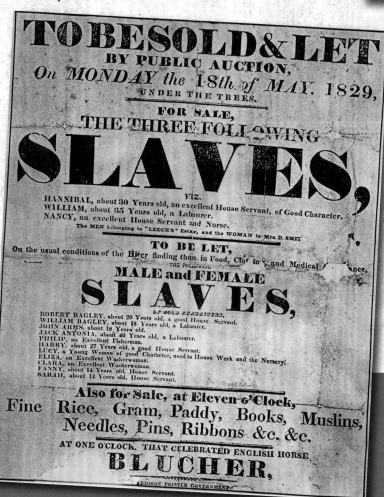

◀ Slave auctions, such as the one advertised in this broadside, were a common way to buy and sell slaves. Sometimes other items were also sold, such as the rice, books, and pins for sale here.

▼ The image below of a group of slaves was made as a stereograph. This used two identical pictures that overlapped about two and a half inches apart. Looking through a device called a stereoscope, the two images combined to make the image look 3D.

EVIDENCE RECORD CARD

A group of "Contrabands" (captured slaves)

LEVEL Primary source
MATERIAL Stereograph
  Photographer: James Gibson
LOCATION Hartford, Connecticut
DATE 1862
SOURCE Library of Congress, Washington, D.C.

VISUAL INFORMATION

Images have always been a great source of information. There have been pictures and decorations on tombs, furniture, and walls for thousands of years. Images are not only a record of an event, they can also help us **visualize** the impact or size of that event.

Before cameras were invented, artists recorded people, places, buildings, and events in paintings, portraits, and sketches. These were sometimes the only record of the way people lived, the landscape, or important events in history.

Photography is a **vital** primary source of information. While artists might express their views or beliefs in what and how they paint a scene or individual, the camera lens gives a more **objective** view.

Primary image sources can be:
- Maps: Diagrams of an area of land
- Photos: Images made by cameras
- Posters: Large printed pictures with or without words
- Billboards: Large outdoor boards showing advertisements
- Flyers and brochures: Small folded pamphlets with pictures and information about products or services

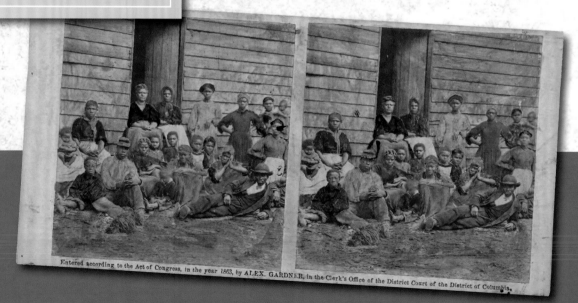

Entered according to the Act of Congress, in the year 1863, by ALEX. GARDNER, in the Clerk's Office of the District Court of the District of Columbia.

- Movies, films, and videos: Stories or events recorded by a camera in a set of moving images

Primary image sources for the Underground Railroad include paintings, illustrations, slave auction flyers, and wanted posters.

Sound is another source of information. We can use tape or digital recorders to capture an event. **Interviews**, speeches, the sound of bombs dropping, or even screaming can bring out powerful emotions in us.

Primary auditory sources can be:
- Music: Sound created by singing or instruments
- Audio recordings: Sound captured on tape, disks, or in computer memory

The **technology** for audio recording did not exist at the time of the Underground Railroad. In later years, interviews and conversations with former slaves, and music from the time of the Underground Railroad were preserved in audio form.

▼This image of a slave auction from 1861 is an engraving. An engraving is a print that was made using a carved pattern in a metal printing plate.

SECONDARY EVIDENCE

Secondary sources are one step further away from the actual event. A secondary source is material created by studying, discussing, and **evaluating** information found in primary sources. Secondary sources often include primary sources such as images. Historians do not consider secondary sources to be as **reliable** as primary sources. Information may be presented in a way that expresses the author's or artist's views and beliefs.

Examples of secondary sources:
- Textbooks: Books used in schools to study a certain subject
- Magazines: Publications that come out on a regular schedule and contain articles and advertisements
- Histories: Books about a certain period of time or event in the past
- Encyclopedias: A set of books that give a little information on many subjects

Many books have been written about slavery and the Underground Railroad. *Uncle Tom's Cabin*, written by Harriet Beecher Stowe, is a fictional story about slavery in the southern United States and some slaves who escaped to freedom in Canada. The author used primary sources, including former slave Josiah Henson's journals, to write her novel. *Uncle Tom's*

135,000 SETS, 270,000 VOLUMES SOLD.

UNCLE TOM'S CABIN

FOR SALE HERE.

AN EDITION FOR THE MILLION, COMPLETE IN 1 Vol., PRICE 37 1-2 CENTS.
" " IN GERMAN, IN 1 Vol., PRICE 50 CENTS.
" " IN 2 Vols,. CLOTH, 6 PLATES, PRICE $1.50.
SUPERB ILLUSTRATED EDITION, IN 1 Vol., WITH 153 ENGRAVINGS,
PRICES FROM $2.50 TO $5.00.

The Greatest Book of the Age.

▲ Harriet Beecher Stowe used the autobiography of the escaped slave Josiah Henson as inspiration for her novel, *Uncle Tom's Cabin.*

"O, missis, do you suppose mas'r would sell my Harry?" And the poor creature threw herself into a chair, and sobbed convulsively. "Sell him! No, you foolish girl! You know your master never deals with those southern traders, and never means to sell any of his servants, as long as they behave well. Why, you silly child, who do you think would want to buy your Harry? Do you think all the

Cabin is a secondary source of information on slavery.

Magazine articles often include images as well as text. For example, to discuss the subject of **abolition**, an article about the life of a slave may include quotations from a person, as well as many pictures. This is an example of a secondary source (the article on slavery) using primary source material (the quotations and pictures) to tell a story.

ANALYZE THIS

Are fictional stories written about events of the Underground Railroad primary sources or secondary sources?

▼ The story and images of escaped slave Gordon, featured in *Harper's Weekly Magazine*, helped **abolitionists** persuade others of the cruelty of slavery.

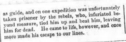

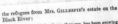

GORDON AS HE ENTERED OUR LINES.

GORDON UNDER MEDICAL INSPECTION.

GORDON IN HIS UNIFORM AS A U. S. SOLDIER

world are set on him as you are, you goosie? Come, cheer up, and hook my dress. There now, put my back hair up in that pretty braid you learnt the other day, and don't go listening at doors any more."

Excerpt from *Uncle Tom's Cabin* by Harriet Beecher Stowe

INTERPRETATION

"Historical research is wildly seductive and fun. There's a thrill in the process of digging, then piecing together details like a puzzle."

Nancy Horan, American author

Historians are a little bit like detectives. They look for clues to past events in lots of different places. They follow trails to find evidence, then they present their findings.

When reading historical material, the reader needs to be aware of **bias**. Bias is **prejudice** in favor of or against one thing, person, or group compared with another. It is usually considered to be unfair. Every person puts a little of himself or herself into their work. Their views, prejudices, or fears might influence them. An artist who supports slavery might portray the slave owner as smiling and kind, and the slaves as happy workers. An artist who is against slavery might choose to paint a scene showing a slave owner cruelly mistreating a slave.

We can also be biased when we study source materials. Two people can see the same thing in two different ways. An image of slaves working on a plantation can be evidence of cruelty to one person, and an example of ordinary working conditions to another person.

Historians are careful to try to recognize bias when analyzing source material. They follow the Bias Rule, which reminds them to read source material critically, to consider the creator's point of view, and to compare it with other sources.

▶ This 18th-century engraving shows black slaves working on a cotton plantation in the West Indies. While slavery was once common worldwide, it is now illegal in all countries.

PERSPECTIVES

Have a close look at this painting. What do you think the bias of the artist is regarding slavery? What clues in the image support this?

fig. 1.

N.º 120
P.RM.

Some sources are less biased than others. Photographs are a true image of what the lens sees, whereas paintings are how an artist sees something. Court documents usually stick to facts, but personal letters are one person's feelings and views. As long as we are aware of bias, it can be seen as an additional source of information on society and culture in the past.

These are the steps historians take in analyzing source material:

- Consider who the author is.
- Consider when the material was created.
- Consider who published it.
- Check what the material contains.
- Consider who the intended audience is.
- Consider how much of the event the source covers.
- Always look for other material to back up sources.

▼ This slave register from 1847 to 1851 shows births on the Good Hope Plantation in Orangeburg, South Carolina. Children born to slave parents were automatically slaves and the property of the slave owner.

ANALYZING CONTEXT

The circumstances or setting in which an event occurs is called the **context**. When analyzing source material, the reader needs to think about what was happening at the time, what the common beliefs were, and what the customs of the area or group were. Posters for slave auctions seem cruel and unbelievable today, but in the context of a time when slavery was common and accepted, a sale of humans was a reason to advertise.

Context can color what an artist or author creates and how we **interpret** events. It can also affect which source materials were saved. The Underground Railroad was a highly secret and dangerous undertaking. Very few records were kept because they could be used as evidence against those people

"A week had passed in terrible suspense, when my pursuers came into such close vicinity that I concluded they had tracked me to my hiding-place. I flew out of the house, and concealed myself in a thicket of bushes."

Excerpt from *Incidents in the Life of a Slave Girl* by Harriet Jacobs

What year is portrayed in this illustration? When was the illustration created? How many years difference are there between the dates? Does this affect how accurate the information might be? What details in the image could be incorrect?

who were helping fugitive slaves. As a result, historians have very few documents to provide information.

When analyzing how valuable source material is, historians use the "time and place" rule. This means that the closer in time and place a source and its creator were to an event, the better the source will be.

From the most reliable to least reliable, they are:
- Direct traces of an event (such as photos).
- Accounts of the event, created at the time of an event by firsthand observers and participants.
- Accounts created after an event by firsthand observers and participants.
- Accounts created after an event by people who did not participate or witness the event, but used interviews or evidence from the time of the event.

▼ As this illustration of 1931 shows, most fugitives stayed hidden during the day and traveled by night. They used the North Star to guide them on their way.

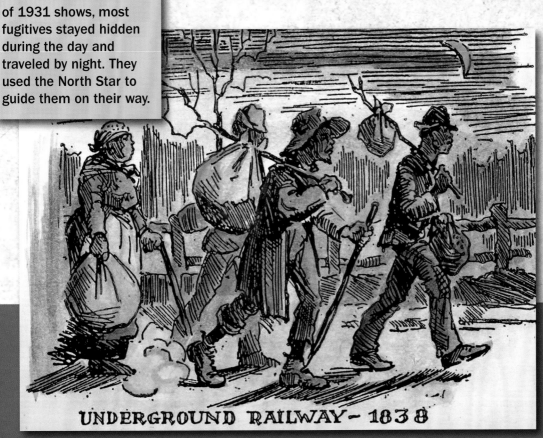

UNDERGROUND RAILWAY – 1838

UNDERGROUND RAILROAD

"I was the conductor of the Underground Railroad for eight years, and I can say what most conductors can't say; I never ran my train off the track and I never lost a passenger."

Harriet Tubman

The Underground Railroad wasn't a railroad, nor was it physically underground. It was a secret system to help fugitive slaves escape to freedom. It used railroad terms to allow people involved to talk to one another in **code**. Different escape routes were called Lines. The free people who helped fugitives were Conductors. Fugitive slaves were called Cargo or Freight. Safe houses along the way were called Stations or Depots.

The Underground Railroad was formed in the early 1800s but reached its peak from 1840 to 1860. Some people estimate that more than 30,000 slaves escaped to Canada during those 20 years. Most slaves headed north, but some went south to Mexico and the Caribbean.

Involvement with the Underground Railroad was dangerous and illegal. Some people involved were abolitionists who did not believe in slavery. Some slaves successfully escaped, then risked their lives to return to help others find freedom. Slaves caught fleeing could be **flogged**, jailed, sold back into slavery, or killed. Conductors could be fined or sent to prison.

▶ The Underground Railroad was not just a series of routes and passwords; it was a system of people helping people.
This oil painting, "The Underground Railroad," was made in 1893 by Charles T. Webber.

ANALYZE THIS

In this painting, look at the people first. How are they dressed? Does this indicate anything about the time of year? Can you guess how old the people are?

Look at objects in the painting. Are people holding things? If you don't know what some of the objects are, ask your teacher or a librarian. Find out how the items were used. What might that tell you?

Look carefully at the buildings and transportation methods. Do they tell you when and where the painting was made?

ANALYZE THIS

How did the abolition movement start in the United States? What were the two ways abolitionists helped free slaves?

Slave catchers were the most feared people along the routes of the Underground Railroad. They were the people who returned slaves to their owners. Sometimes they roamed the countryside in gangs, and they often used **bloodhounds** to track down their prey.

The Fugitive Slave Act of 1793 gave slave owners the right to have their slaves returned. It also made helping runaways and fugitives a crime. In 1850, this act was strengthened to add that it was the duty of even ordinary free citizens to help return runaway slaves to their owners. It also meant that slave catchers could pursue and capture fugitives in places where they would legally be free.

ABOLITIONISTS

Slave catchers had their own enemies. These were the abolitionists. Abolitionists **defied** the Fugitive Slave Act and refused to help slave catchers, sometimes even hiding slaves in their own homes and carriages.

The abolitionist movement started with a religious group called the **Quakers**. Quakers are Christians who believe in social justice. They soon convinced others that keeping people as slaves was wrong. With Western Europe, including Britain and its colony of Canada, already making slavery illegal, they pushed for the same change in the United States.

▼ Abolitionists not only helped slaves escape, but they also convinced many slave owners to willingly free their slaves.

"A person informed Slator that he had met a man and woman, in a trap, answering to the description of those whom he had lost, driving furiously towards Savannah. So Slator and several slavehunters on horseback started off in full tilt, with their bloodhounds, in pursuit of Frank and Mary."

Excerpt from *Running a Thousand Miles to Freedom* by William and Ellen Craft

▲ Many escaped slaves, such as Frederick Douglass (seated, front left), attended the Fugitive Slave Law Convention held in 1850 in Cazenovia, New York, to protest the Fugitive Slave Act.

The flight to freedom for a fugitive slave was an exhausting, **perilous** risk. If a slave trusted the wrong person along the way and was caught, the punishment was swift, brutal, and often fatal.

William Still was an abolitionist who was one of the few who dared keep records of the people he helped. By studying this primary source, we can see that most escapees were men traveling alone. That was the safest way to stay quiet and well hidden. More people meant more danger.

Josiah Henson was an **exception**. He was a slave from Maryland who escaped to Canada with his wife and four children. His autobiography of his journey revealed details about life on the run.

▼ Traveling on foot was slow and often tiring. Conductors would try to secure wagons to move the fugitive slaves across country more quickly.

DANGERS ON THE JOURNEY

Fugitive slaves, whether alone or with their families, carried very little with them. Most of the time, they left with only the clothes on their backs. They faced starvation along the way, eating only the food they could **scavenge** from gardens or beg from supporters. The weather grew colder the farther north they traveled. They were not used to such low temperatures. Quite often, the tattered clothes they wore were not good protection.

"*The chief practical difficulty that had weighed upon my mind, was connected with the youngest two of the children. They were of three and two years, respectively, and of course would have to be carried. Both stout and healthy, they were a heavy burden, and my wife had declared that I should break down under it before I had got five miles from home.*"

Excerpt from *Truth Stranger than Fiction* by Josiah Henson

Fugitives had to travel hundreds of miles on foot. Most would stay hidden during the day and travel at night, letting the darkness give them cover. Wild animals were a concern, especially those that hunted at night. And if a fugitive did get injured or sick on that long journey, there was little help.

Slave owners knew that stories of slaves who made it to freedom could encourage their own slaves to try to escape. If they could read and write, slaves were not allowed to send or receive letters and they were not allowed to gather in groups, except for church. Church became their lifeline. Gossip, stories, and even hymns became ways to share information and instructions.

ANALYZE THIS

Most slaves could not read or write. In what other ways were slaves able to share information secretly?

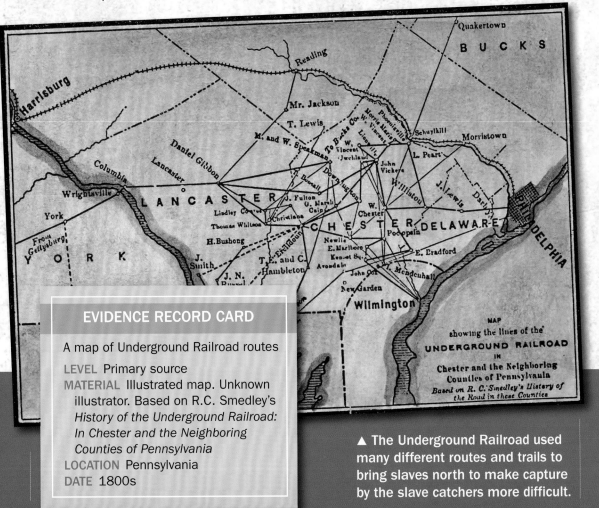

EVIDENCE RECORD CARD

A map of Underground Railroad routes

LEVEL Primary source
MATERIAL Illustrated map. Unknown illustrator. Based on R.C. Smedley's *History of the Underground Railroad: In Chester and the Neighboring Counties of Pennsylvania*
LOCATION Pennsylvania
DATE 1800s

▲ The Underground Railroad used many different routes and trails to bring slaves north to make capture by the slave catchers more difficult.

THE STORY OF HARRIET TUBMAN

One of the most famous Underground Railroad conductors was Harriet Tubman. She was born into slavery in Maryland in about 1820. Harriet watched in horror as her older sisters were sold, splitting the family forever. When her mother stopped the sale of a younger brother by hiding him for a month, the idea grew in Harriet of **resistance** against slavery and being able to change her future.

In 1849, Harriet escaped. She fled from Maryland to Pennsylvania, which was a **free state**, or a state without slavery. There she did odd jobs and saved her money, trying to start a new life. She learned that some family members were being sold at a slave auction in Massachusetts. She decided to help them escape.

That was the beginning of Harriet's **crusade** to help others find the freedom that she had. As an escaped slave, it was extremely risky. She used many types of tricks to avoid being seen by slave catchers. She carried chickens to pretend to be running errands, or hid her face on a train by pretending to read a newspaper.

She made trips south for 10 years, helping more than 300 slaves, including her parents and brothers, escape. She also left instructions that allowed another 60 or more slaves to find their way to Canada. Her work leading enslaved people to freedom earned her the nickname "Moses."

▶ Slave owners in Maryland never knew that it was a small, determined slave who was encouraging their slaves to make a run for freedom. They believed it must be a white abolitionist from the North.

"When I found I had crossed that line [into Pennsylvania], I looked at my hands to see if I was the same person. There was such a glory over everything; the sun came like gold through the trees, and over the fields, and I felt like I was in Heaven."

Harriet Tubman

PERSPECTIVES

This image shows a group of slaves on the Underground Railroad. Find details in the painting that reflect some of the things that made the journey dangerous.

▲ Harriet usually helped slaves escape in the winter because the cold weather kept people indoors. She also left on Saturdays because reward advertisements wouldn't come out until the Monday papers.

ESCAPE PLANS

With thousands of slaves coming from so many different areas, the Underground Railroad needed many conductors and stations to work.

John Fairfield grew up in a family that owned slaves in Virginia, but he disagreed with slavery. As a young man, he helped a friend who was a slave escape from his uncle's farm. After that, he became involved with the abolitionists and came up with plans to help slaves escape. Once, he got 28 slaves out of the area by hiding them in the coaches of a funeral **procession**.

William Still is called the "Father of the Underground Railroad." William was the youngest of 18 children, and both his parents were slaves. But his father managed to buy his freedom and his mother escaped to freedom. He knew very well what the horrors of a life of slavery were, and he spent his life helping others to escape—often more than 50 slaves a month. He kept very detailed records of the people he helped, and those diaries are some of the best primary evidence there is for the Underground Railroad.

MAINLINE STATION

Levi Coffin was a Quaker who lived in Indiana. His businesses made him wealthy, and he used his money to provide supplies for the fugitive slaves. His house was a station along the railroad. So many slaves hid out there on their journey north, that it was called the

▲ Like most formerly enslaved peoples, William Still had no formal education as a child, but he achieved the amazing feat of teaching himself to read and write as an adult. He used his new skills to write letters of protest and even publish his own book that told the stories of the slaves he helped.

"We want to give you some clean clothing, but you need washing before putting them on. It will make you feel like a new man to have the dirt of slavery all washed off."

Excerpt from the diary of William Still

$150 REWARD

RANAWAY from the subscriber, on the night of the 2d instant, a negro man, who calls himself *Henry May*, about 22 years old, 5 feet 6 or 8 inches high, ordinary color, rather chunky built, bushy head, and has it divided mostly on one side, and keeps it very nicely combed; has been raised in the house, and is a first rate dining-room servant, and was in a tavern in Louisville for 18 months. I expect he is now in Louisville trying to make his escape to a free state, (in all probability to Cincinnati, Ohio.) Perhaps he may try to get employment on a steamboat. He is a good cook, and is handy in any capacity as a house servant. Had on when he left, a dark cassinett coatee, and dark striped cassinett pantaloons, new—he had other clothing. I will give $50 reward if taken in Louisvill; 100 dollars if taken one hundred miles from Louisville in this State, and 150 dollars if taken out of this State, and delivered to me, or secured in any jail so that I can get him again.

WILLIAM BURKE.

Bardstown, Ky., September 3d, 1838.

◄ Because notices such as these mentioned what slaves were wearing and where they might be headed, conductors made sure to give them new clothes and send them in another direction.

▼ Slaves who stopped at the Johnson House in Germantown, Pennsylvania, for food and rest, hid in the third-floor attic.

ANALYZE THIS

Is a diary entry written about events of the Underground Railroad a primary source or secondary source?

Quotations can explain the reasons for someone's actions:

"The Bible, in bidding us to feed the hungry and clothe the naked, said nothing about color, and I should try to follow out the teachings of that good book."

Levi Coffin

Cargo or freight were the code words used for fugitive slaves using the Underground Railroad. These brave men and women took extraordinary measures to find their own freedom.

Harriet Jacobs was born a slave in 1813 in North Carolina. Because her owner died, she was handed over to a doctor who began to abuse her. She turned for comfort to a white lawyer named Samuel Sawyer. She had two children with him. Not able to stop the abuse by her owner, she decided to leave her children to the care of Sawyer and escape.

A SECRET HIDING PLACE

Harriet Jacobs wrote about her difficult life in an autobiography called *Incidents in the Life of a Slave Girl*. In it, she explains that before she could make her way along the Underground Railroad, she hid for seven years in a tiny **crawlspace** over the front door of her grandmother's house. She finally escaped to Pennsylvania in 1842.

Ellen and William Craft were both slaves living in Georgia. They met and married in 1846 but couldn't live together because they were owned by different masters. They began to plan an escape so they could be free and

▲ When Josiah Henson reached Ontario, Canada, he helped to found Dawn Settlement. This 200-acre area became a self-sufficient community for escaped slaves.

"Countless were the nights that I sat late at the little loophole scarcely large enough to give me a glimpse of one twinkling star. There, heard the patrols and slave-hunters conferring together about the capture of runaways, well knowing how rejoiced they would be to catch me."

Excerpt from *Incidents in the Life of a Slave Girl* by Harriet Jacobs

live together as a family. Ellen was the daughter of a slave woman and a white man. She had a very pale **complexion** and could pass as a white woman. They made a daring plan. Because slave catchers looked for a man and woman, Ellen cut her hair, put on men's clothes, and bandaged her chin as if she had a toothache to hide her feminine looks.

Her husband acted like her slave. They traveled right under the noses of slave catchers on trains and boats until they reached Boston, where abolitionists found them a place to stay. They eventually moved to England, where they published their story in a book called *Running a Thousand Miles to Freedom.*

▼ Henry Brown was shipped in a box by the Adams Express company on March 23, 1849. The box was labeled "dry goods." It was lined with a cloth and had one hole cut in the top for air. The trip took 27 hours.

THE RESURRECTION OF HENRY BOX BROWN AT PHILADELPHIA.
Who escaped from Richmond Va in a Box 3 feet long 2½ ft deep and 2 ft wide

ANALYZE THIS

Think like a historian

How can researchers really know what some people in the past lived through? Some historians try to recreate events to get a better understanding. Historian Anthony Cohen heard about slave Henry Brown, who packed himself in a crate and mailed himself to freedom. Cohen wanted to test this to see if it was possible. He and his friends built a crate big enough that he could sit with his legs close to his chest. It had air holes covered with stickers that he could poke through to breathe. He found it hot and scary and was relieved to step out. It helped him understand the fear, anxiety, and desperation slaves must have felt.

EVIDENCE REVISTED

"You never really understand a person until you consider things from his point of view... until you climb inside of his skin and walk around in it."

In *To Kill a Mockingbird*, by Harper Lee

PERSPECTIVES

How would you feel if you were a runaway slave and you saw the poster opposite? How would you feel if you were a slave owner or slave catcher?

Each person who lived through or lived during the time of the Underground Railroad had a different view of what happened. Reading a variety of materials is the best way to get a more complete understanding of this time in history.

The view of slavery and fugitive slaves was very different between people living in the northern and people living in the southern states.

DIVIDED OPINIONS

Northern states were free states. Most people were against slavery, but some did not want to get involved. Abolitionists were much more **vocal** and stepped up to help slaves with their escape to freedom by offering their homes as safe houses. We can get an idea of how they felt by looking at primary source material, such as warning posters, which alerted fugitive slaves that slave catchers were in the area.

For those living in the southern states, slavery was a normal way of life. They believed that slaves were a necessary part of running their farms and **plantations**. Without them, they could not afford to supply the country with crops and cotton. Newspaper advertisements offered rewards for the return of slaves to their owners.

▶ Fugitive slaves escaping from Cambridge, Maryland, at the start of the dangerous journey north to freedom.

CAUTION!!

COLORED PEOPLE
OF BOSTON, ONE & ALL,

You are hereby respectfully CAUTIONED and advised, to avoid conversing with the

Watchmen and Police Officers of Boston,

For since the recent ORDER OF THE MAYOR & ALDERMEN, they are empowered to act as

KIDNAPPERS
AND
Slave Catchers,

And they have already been actually employed in KIDNAPPING, CATCHING, AND KEEPING SLAVES. Therefore, if you value your LIBERTY, and the *Welfare of the Fugitives* among you, *Shun* them in every possible manner, as so many *HOUNDS* on the track of the most unfortunate of your race.

Keep a Sharp Look Out for KIDNAPPERS, and have TOP EYE open.

APRIL 24, 1851.

EVIDENCE RECORD CARD

A runaway slave handbill
LEVEL Primary source
MATERIAL Printed poster
   Creator: Theodore Parker
LOCATION Boston, Massachusetts
DATE April 24, 1851
SOURCE The Granger Collection

▲ While slave owners posted flyers offering rewards for runaway slaves, abolitionists posted their own flyers warning fugitive slaves about slave catchers.

ESCAPE STORY

Primary and secondary source materials also show the different viewpoints of the Underground Railroad between slaves and slave owners.

Slaves risked their lives to escape a life of **bondage**. Some of their journals and letters paint a picture of a desperate life full of **separation** from family and cruelty from masters. They yearn to be free and are willing to undergo the most dangerous journey of their lives to obtain that freedom.

In former slave William Green's firsthand account of his escape, he tells how he faced hunger, drowning, and a near capture several times before he finally reached New York and a chance to build a new life for himself.

"We lay down to take a little rest, and when we awoke we found to our consternation that we were right behind a fodder house, and the men were then out feeding. We crept away as slyly as we could, and got into the main road without any one seeing us. It was very foggy when we went into the woods, and that is the reason we did not know we were so near any house; however, we got out of this difficulty."

From the autobiography of William Green, *Narrative of Events in the Life of William Green*

CONCERNED OWNERS

Slave owners were worried that their entire workforce would leave them. They believed that slaves were **essential** to run their

ANALYZE THIS

Read the excerpt from Henry Tayloe's letter below. What does this section tell you about how slave owners viewed their slaves?

"The present high price of Negroes can not continue long and if you will make me a partner in the sale on reasonable terms I will bring them out this Fall from VA and sell them for you and release you from all troubles."

Letter from Henry Tayloe to his brother B.O. Tayloe

▲Daniel Osborn was a Quaker living in Ohio. This page from his diary is a rare record of the many people he helped along the Underground Railroad.

plantations and bring in the crops. They felt that slaves were their "property" and should be returned to them.

For slave owners, the Underground Railroad was a source of frustration. With slaves leaving in record numbers, their source of free labor was disappearing. They were desperate to keep what they believed was their property—their slaves. They posted rewards for the return of slaves and **petitioned** the courts to punish the people responsible for helping them escape.

EVIDENCE RECORD CARD

Idealized portrait of American slavery
LEVEL Primary source
MATERIAL Print on woven paper. Artist: Edward Williams Clay
LOCATION Southern United States
DATE 1841
SOURCE Library of Congress

AMERICA

God bless you massa! you feed and clothe us. When we are sick you nurse us, and when too old to work, you provide for us!

These poor creatures are a sacred legacy from my ancestors and while a dollar is left me, nothing shall be spared to increase their comfort and happiness.

◀ Slave owners believed they were doing blacks a favor by giving them shelter and food in exchange for honest work.

Sometimes facts from history are **exaggerated** or even completely made up. Looking at source material is a way to find the truth behind myths.

Some people believe that slaves used hymn lyrics in church to pass on information. While historians know that slaves used church gatherings to trade gossip and stories, did they really use lyrics to give slaves thinking of escape a roadmap to the North? Looking at source material can help unravel the mystery.

Follow the Drinking Gourd and *Swing Low, Sweet Chariot* are two songs that some say had ties to the Underground Railroad. *Follow the Drinking Gourd* was first collected in 1910 by H.B. Parks. He said that a man named Peg Leg Joe spread the song while he worked on plantations in the South. Translated lyrics from the song, such as "The riverbank makes a very good road," "The river ends between two hills," and "When the great big river meets the little river" may be directions. The "drinking gourd" might be code for the group of stars called "The Big Dipper."

Historians are not convinced. They say that in the area where this song originated, slaves mostly fled to the South, not to the North. They argue that such exact directions meant that slave catchers could lie in wait on routes that would be used over and over again. The Underground Railroad always used different

SONG LYRICS

Read the lyrics to *Swing Low, Sweet Chariot* here: www.negrospirituals.com/ news-song/swing_low_ sweet_chariot_swing_ lo.htm

Then listen to a recording by the Fisk Jubilee Singers: www.youtube.com/ watch?v=GUvBGZnL9rE

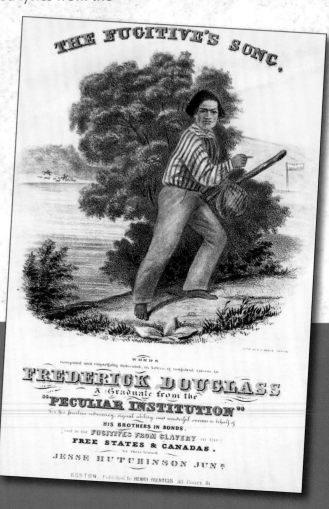

▶ *The Fugitive's Song* was written as a tribute to abolitionist Frederick Douglass by Jesse Hutchinson Junior. The cover shows Douglass as a runaway slave.

ANALYZE THIS

Do you think there is enough evidence in source materials to prove that the lyrics for *Follow the Drinking Gourd* were used as coded messages for the Underground Railroad? What about the lyrics for *Swing Low, Sweet Chariot*?

routes for safety. Some doubt the song's authenticity.

Information about the author of the song, *Swing Low, Sweet Chariot*, was gathered by historian Mabel Alexander. She learned that a slave wrote the song and lyrics before 1862. It was sung for Queen Victoria by the Fisk Jubilee Singers in 1873. These dates fit with the time that slaves used the railroad. It was known to be one of Harriet Tubman's favorite hymns. Some slaves changed the lyrics to: "Swing Low, Sweet Harriet."

▲ The **Emancipation Proclamation** by Missouri governor Thomas C. Fletcher was made in 1865. Slaves in some states did not realize that President Lincoln had made his Emancipation Proclamation two years earlier, in 1863. Slaves celebrate Juneteenth to remember June 19, 1865, the day they found out.

HISTORY REPEATED

*"Freedom means you are **unobstructed** in living your life as you choose. Anything less is a form of slavery."*

Dr. Wayne Dyer, American psychologist

Slavery has many forms. Today's slavery involves people brought to foreign countries to be maids, **prostitutes**, and servants, and to work in salons, factories, farms, and massage parlors. Sometimes, the person has been kidnapped and forced into a life of slavery. Other times, they are working off a debt to someone who helped them flee from another country.

TRAFFICKING

The National **Human Trafficking** Resource Center (NHTRC) was founded to fight modern slavery. Human trafficking is the act of illegally moving people to hold them in forced labor. The NHTRC helps people who find themselves held in forced labor to escape. Just like the conductors on the Underground Railroad, volunteers give up weekends, holidays, and even sleep to make sure every call for help gets answered.

Like the warning posters posted by abolitionists that slave catchers were in the area, the NHTRC has a pamphlet called "Know Your Rights" that lists things to look out for and includes the toll-free number. In just five years, the NHTRC received reports of more than 9,000 cases of human trafficking in the United States.

Victims of human trafficking get help to find a place to stay, to hire lawyers to deal with their immigration papers, start classes to learn job skills and improve their English, and even how to press charges against their abusers.

PROTECTION FOR WORKERS!

ACCOUNTABILITY FOR TRAFFICKERS

Damayan Migrant Workers Association
damayanmpinsa.org

BREAK FREE FROM LABOR TRAFFICKING END DOMESTIC SLAVERY!

Damayan Migrant Workers Assocation
dama

ANALYZE THIS

Even though slavery is illegal, name two ways people today might end up as modern slaves.

◀ Human trafficking is the second-largest and the fastest-growing criminal industry in the world. Protestors call on governments to make laws tighter and punishments tougher.

A NEW UNDERGROUND RAILROAD

Those trying to flee **repressive** countries sometimes use a network of escape routes and safe houses similar to the Underground Railroad. North Korea is one of the most isolated countries in the world. Each year, a few brave people try to escape using "Asia's Underground Railroad."

The difficulty for the people using Asia's Underground Railroad is that many must first escape to China. China is not a free country and, in fact, has political ties to North Korea. Even after fugitives make it across the border, they are still not safe. They must stay in hiding because, if they are found by Chinese officials, they will be sent back. Many North Koreans spend days, months, or even years trying to find a way out of China to South Korea or other south Asian countries.

Like the system in North America, Asia's Underground Railroad has safe houses, secret routes, and conductors. Some conductors are **missionaries** wanting to do good work; others are **brokers**. Brokers help escapees for a price. Like many black slaves who escaped then returned to help others, some conductors on this underground railroad are Koreans who have found freedom and return to help others. It is extremely dangerous because people who are caught can face severe punishments, even death. So far, about 25,000 people have escaped from North Korea.

Author Melanie Kirkpatrick has written a book, called *Escape from North Korea*, which tells the stories of people who have managed to escape.

▲ Once in China, North Koreans stand out. They are often sick, injured, or hungry. Conductors give them food, clothing, and medicine to help them blend in.

ANALYZE THIS

Is Melanie Kirkpatrick's book, *Escape from North Korea*, a primary or secondary source? How do you know?

We are able to see the context of someone's actions through their words:

"In 1939, they were forced to wear Jewish stars, and people were herded and shut up into ghettos...With people behaving like pigs, I felt the Jews were being destroyed. I had to help them. There was no choice."

Oskar Schindler

▲ A migrant worker moves from place to place to find work. Farm workers are often held as "debt slaves" who have to pay back crew leaders for their ride to the region.

TIMELINE

1513 Juan Ponce de León sees Florida for the first time

1550

1581 The first African slaves are imported in St. Augustine, Florida

1600

1607 John Smith founds the Jamestown settlement in Virginia

1619 About 20 Africans brought to Jamestown, Virginia, are the first slaves shipped to Britain's North American colonies

1650

1662 A law in Virginia states that the children born to slave mothers inherit her slave status

1700

1705 Virginia law describes slaves as property, allowing them to be willed to new owners and permitting owners to "kill and destroy" runaways

1712 A slave revolt takes place in New York on April 7: nine whites are killed and 21 slaves executed

1750

1773 Slaves in Massachusetts petition the government for freedom: they are turned down

1775 The first abolitionist society is founded by Anthony Benezet of Philadelphia, Pennsylvania

1793 The Fugitive Slave Act gives slave owners the right to find, capture, and bring back escaped slaves

1794 Eli Whitney invents the cotton gin, making cotton a profitable product; this creates a huge demand for slave labor

1800

1808 The United States bans importing African slaves, but many are still smuggled into the country

1812 The War of 1812 begins between the United States and Britain

1820 The Missouri Compromise is a law that declares that slavery is forbidden in northern states but allowed in southern states

1847 William Still begins working as a clerk for the Pennsylvania Anti-Slavery Society

1849 Harriet Tubman escapes slavery in Maryland; she returns 19 times to help others, including her family, to escape

1850

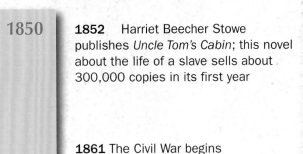

1850 The Fugitive Slave Law gives slave catchers the right to recapture slaves even in free states, and makes it the duty of all citizens to help return slaves to their owners

1852 Harriet Beecher Stowe publishes *Uncle Tom's Cabin*; this novel about the life of a slave sells about 300,000 copies in its first year

1859 John Brown and 21 others launch a slave revolt at Harpers Ferry

1861 The Civil War begins

1863 President Lincoln issues the Emancipation Proclamation that declares that all persons held as slaves would now be free

1865 The Thirteenth Amendment to the Constitution is passed, outlawing slavery

Map of eastern North America showing Underground Railroad routes, slave and free states.

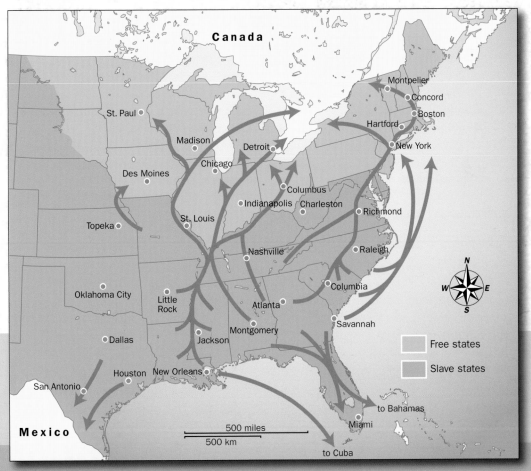

BIBLIOGRAPHY

QUOTATIONS AND EXCERPTS

p.4 George Santayana quote: *The Life of Reason: Reason in Common Sense.* Scribner's, 1905.

pp.6, 24 Josiah Henson quotes: *Truth Stranger than Fiction: Father Henson's Story of His Own Life.* Barnes & Noble Library of Essential Reading, 2008.

p.8 C. William Pollard quote: *The Soul of the Firm.* Zondervan, 2000.

pp.8, 22 Craft, William, and Ellen Craft. *Running a Thousand Miles to Freedom: Or, the Escape of William and Ellen Craft from Slavery.* Dover Publications, 2014.

pp.10, 28 William Still quotes: *The Underground Railroad: Authentic Narratives and First-Hand Accounts.* Dover Publications, 2007.

p.11 Abraham Lincoln quote: http://www.abrahamlincolnonline.org/lincoln/speeches/pierce.htm

pp.14–15 Stowe, Harriet Beecher. *Uncle Tom's Cabin.* Townsend Press, 2006.

p.16 Nancy Horan quote: *Craving Stories,* http://www.powells.com/essays/horan.html

pp.18, 30 Harriet Jacobs quotes: *Incidents in the Life of a Slave Girl.* Oshun Publishing Company, 2013.

pp.20, 26 Harriet Tubman quotes: Clinton, Catherine. *Harriet Tubman, The Road to Freedom.* Back Bay Books, 2005.

p.29 Levi Coffin quote: *Reminiscences of Levi Coffin, The Reputed President of the Underground Railroad.* Western Tract Society, 1876.

p. 32 Lee, Harper. *To Kill a Mockingbird.* Grand Central Publishing, 1988.

p.34 William Green quote: *Narrative of Events in the Life of William Green, (formerly a slave).* Cornell University Library, 1853.

p.34 Henry Tayloe quote: http://ci.columbia.edu/hkc/proto2/eseminars/0751_dbq1.html#docc

p.38 Wayne Dyer quote: *Pulling Your Own Strings.* HarperCollins, 2001.

p.40 Oskar Schindler quote: from a 1964 interview in front of his apartment in West Germany http://www.schindlerjews.com/

INTERNET GUIDELINES

Finding good source material on the Internet can sometimes be a challenge. Analyze each site you find and check out the information on it. How reliable is it?

- Who is the author of the page? Is it an expert in the field, or a person who experienced the event?
- Is the site well known and up to date? A page that has not been updated for several years probably has out-of-date information.
- Can you verify the facts with another site? Always double-check information.

- Have you checked all possible sites? Don't just look on the first page a search engine provides. Remember to try government sites and research papers.
- Have you recorded website addresses and names? Keep this data so you can backtrack and verify the information you want to use.

TO FIND OUT MORE

Non-Fiction:
Carson, Mary Kay. *The Underground Railroad for Kids: From Slavery to Freedom with 21 Activities.* Chicago Review Press, 2005.

Kirkpatrick, Melanie. *Escape from North Korea: The Untold Story of Asia's Underground Railroad.* Encounter Books, 2014.

Petry, Ann. *Harriet Tubman: Conductor on the Underground Railroad.* Amistad, 2007.

Sterling, Dorothy. *Freedom Train: The Story of Harriet Tubman.* Scholastic Inc., 1991.

Historical Fiction:
Bradford, Karleen. *A Desperate Road to Freedom* (Dear Canada). Scholastic Canada, 2009.

Greenwood, Barbara. *The Last Safe House: A Story of the Underground Railroad.* Kids Can Press, 1998.

McKissack, Patricia C. *A Picture of Freedom* (Dear America). Scholastic Press, 2011.

Stowe, Harriet Beecher. *Uncle Tom's Cabin.* Dover Publications, 2005.

Wyeth, Sharon Dennis. *Freedom's Wings* (My America). Scholastic Inc., 2002.

WEBSITES AND MULTIMEDIA

The Discovery Channel presents a series of videos on slavery:
www.discovery.com/tv-shows/other-shows/videos/assignment-discovery-underground-railroad.htm

An interactive website on the Underground Railroad:
http://teacher.scholastic.com/activities/bhistory/underground_railroad/

Ducksters answers questions on the Underground Railroad:
www.ducksters.com/history/civil_war/underground_railroad.php

National Geographic—Play The Underground Railroad: Journey to Freedom game:
http://education.nationalgeographic.com/education/media/underground-railroad-journey-freedom/?ar_a=1

An interactive map to explore routes of the Underground Railroad:
http://eduplace.com/kids/socsci/books/applications/imaps/maps/g5s_u6/

African American Migration Experience: The Transatlantic Slave Trade
www.inmotionaame.org/migrations/landing.cfm?migration=1

GLOSSARY

abolition The act of officially ending or stopping something

abolitionists People who did not believe in slavery and wanted to abolish it

age A distinct period of history

artifacts Objects of historical interest made by humans

auction A public sale where goods—including slaves—are sold to the highest bidder

audio recording A recording of sounds or voices on tape or disk

auditory Using the sense of hearing

beliefs Things accepted as truths

bias Prejudice in favor of or against one thing, person, or group

bloodhound A breed of dog with a very keen sense of smell

bondage The state of being a slave

broker Someone who helps other people for money

century 100 years

characteristic A feature or trait of a particular person, place, or thing

circumstance A fact or event that makes a situation the way it is

code A system of signs and secret writings to keep a message secret

complexion The natural color and texture of a person's skin

context The circumstances or setting in which an event happens

crawlspace A small space under a roof or floor

crusade A fight to change a social, political, or religious issue

culture The arts and other achievements of a society

decade A period of ten years

defied Openly refused to obey

Emancipation Proclamation The order issued by President Lincoln in 1863 to free all slaves in the United States

era A long period of history, with a distinct characteristic

essential Necessary

evaluating Forming an idea about

evidence The body of facts or information to show whether something is true

exaggerated Represented as larger, better, or worse than it really is

exception Something or someone that does not fit a general rule

excerpt An extract or short passage from a book, movie, or other production

flogged Beaten with a whip or stick as punishment

free state An American state without slavery or slaves

fugitives People who escape, or are in hiding

generation All the people born and living at the same time

historian A person who studies history

history Past events and their description

human trafficking Illegally moving people to hold them in forced labor

insight A deep understanding of a person or thing

interpret To explain the meaning of something

interview A meeting with a person by a reporter, journalist, or recorder to get facts

involvement Having taken part in something

lyrics The words of a song

memorabilia Small objects connected with special people or events

millennium A period of 1,000 years

missionaries People sent to another country or region on a religious mission

objective Not taking sides

orally Spoken; told with words

papyrus Paper made in Egypt from the stem of a water plant

parchment Stiff, flat material made from animal skins

perilous Full of danger or risk

petitioned Asked for something formally

plantation A huge estate on which crops are grown

prejudice An opinion formed before learning the facts

preserved Kept in its original condition

primary source A firsthand account or direct evidence of an event

procession A group of people or vehicles moving in a parade

prostitute A person who participates in sexual activities for money

Quaker Member of the Christian movement, the Religious Society of Friends

quotation Written or spoken words repeated in a later work, speech, or conversation

reliable Something that can be trusted

repressive Preventing the freedom of people

resistance Refusing to go along with something

scavenge To look for things in other people's trash

secondary source Material created by studying primary sources

separation Moving or being moved apart

social media Websites and applications that let people create and share information

society A group of people forming a single community with its own distinctive culture and institutions

source Original document or other piece of evidence

technology Equipment developed through scientific knowledge

unobstructed Not blocked in any way

vellum A fine paper, once made from animal skin

visualize To see things in your mind

vital Absolutely necessary

vocal Expressing feelings freely or loudly